Checks and Balances
Creating the
United States Government

M. M. Eboch

Series Editor
Mark Pearcy

Contents

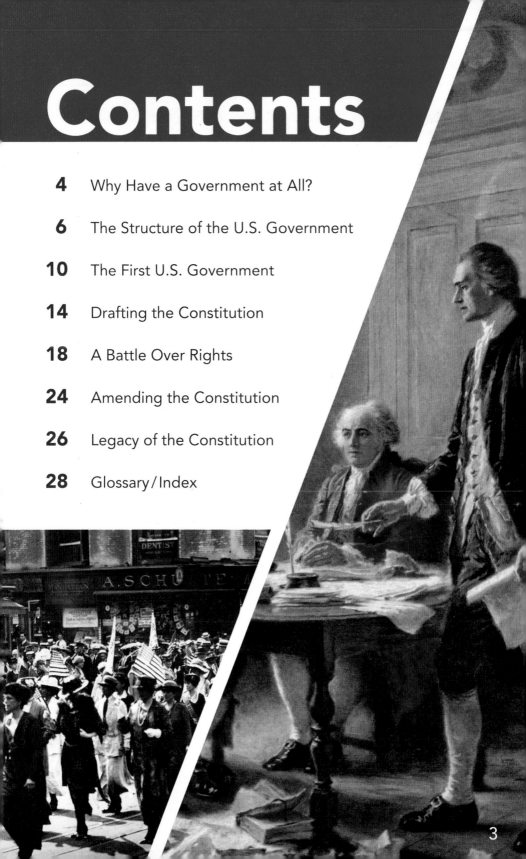

Why Have a Government at All?

A government is a system of authority that rules over a country or a state. Having a government means having to obey rules set by other people. Have you ever wondered why people would be willing to live with so many rules?

Governments have many duties and serve many functions. In the United States, the set of laws that explains the structure, duties, and powers of the government is called the Constitution. According to the Constitution, the government's purpose is to create, defend, interpret, and **enforce** rules — or laws — in order to protect the stability of society and the rights of the people. To prevent any one group in government from having too much power, the Constitution divides the government into three main branches. It gives each branch the power to restrain, or hold back, the others. This system is called Checks and Balances.

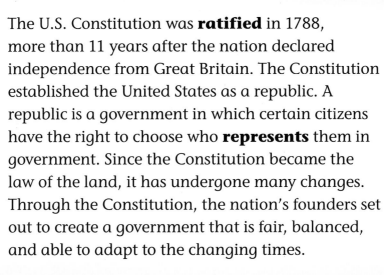

The U.S. Constitution was **ratified** in 1788, more than 11 years after the nation declared independence from Great Britain. The Constitution established the United States as a republic. A republic is a government in which certain citizens have the right to choose who **represents** them in government. Since the Constitution became the law of the land, it has undergone many changes. Through the Constitution, the nation's founders set out to create a government that is fair, balanced, and able to adapt to the changing times.

The U.S. Capitol building is where Congress meets.

The Structure of the U.S. Government

The U.S. government is divided into three main branches, each with its own powers and responsibilities.

The Three Branches

The legislative branch, or Congress, makes the nation's laws. It also has the power to declare war and determine the federal budget. Under the Constitution, Congress is divided into two bodies of legislative governance: the Senate and the House of Representatives. For a law to be passed, both houses have to agree to it.

The executive branch is led by the office of the president. It consists of the office of the vice-president, the president's cabinet members, or advisers, and various federal agencies. The executive branch is in charge of enforcing the laws.

The judicial branch is made up of the Supreme Court and lower federal courts. Currently, the authority of the Supreme Court lies among nine justices, or judges. Among its other powers, the Supreme Court is in charge of determining whether laws are valid according to the Constitution.

The Supreme Court building in Washington, D.C.

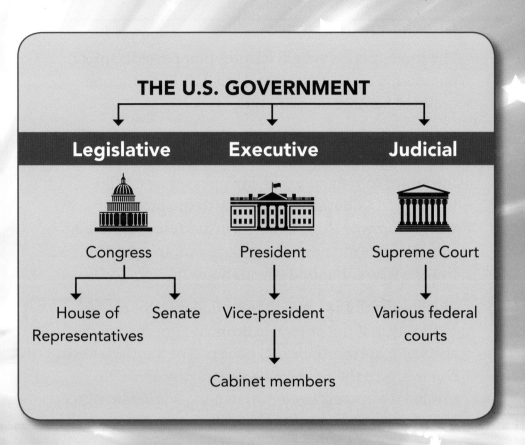

THE U.S. GOVERNMENT

Legislative

Congress

House of Representatives · Senate

Executive

President

Vice-president

Cabinet members

Judicial

Supreme Court

Various federal courts

For Your Information

The president can also issue commands directly to federal agencies without Congress's permission. These commands are called executive orders. Although executive orders are not mentioned specifically in the Constitution, they have been used by all but one president.

Checks and Balances

The three-branch system ensures that power is spread out among three groups, making it difficult for one group to become too powerful.

Even though the legislative branch — Congress — is in charge of proposing and writing laws, the president has the power to veto, or reject, laws passed by Congress. However, if Congress disagrees with the president's veto, it can vote to override it. Furthermore, although Congress has the power to declare war, the president is the one who commands the nation's military forces.

The president's office may seem to hold a lot of authority, but the other two branches are constantly checking, or controlling, its powers. The Supreme Court can overturn the president's executive orders. The president appoints leaders of major government offices and Supreme Court justices, but it is up to Congress to approve or reject these appointments. Congress even has the power to remove the president from office in a process called impeachment.

The White House is the home and workplace of the president.

Congress can impeach Supreme Court justices as well. However, the Supreme Court has the power to interpret laws passed by Congress and overturn those it believes to be **contrary** to the Constitution. The Supreme Court does not have the power to change the law. Any changes to the Constitution must come from the legislative branch.

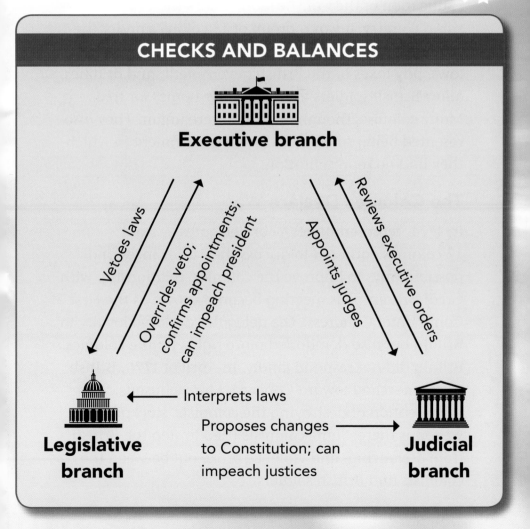

CHECKS AND BALANCES

Executive branch

Vetoes laws

Overrides veto; confirms appointments; can impeach president

Appoints judges

Reviews executive orders

Legislative branch

Interprets laws

Proposes changes to Constitution; can impeach justices

Judicial branch

The First U.S. Government

The creation of the U.S. government was neither fast nor simple. Many events led to the writing and ratification of the Constitution. Before the United States was a country, it was a group of 13 colonies under the rule of Great Britain. The colonists had to obey Britain's laws, pay taxes to the British government, and at times, allow British soldiers to stay in their homes for free. Many colonists thought the laws were unfair. They also resented being ruled by a distant government in which they had no representation.

The Colonies Declare War

In 1774, representatives — or delegates — from 12 colonies gathered to discuss their grievances and possible ways to improve the colonies' relationship with Great Britain. This meeting became known as the First Continental Congress. The delegates declared loyalty to Britain but also demanded more rights for the colonies. Britain did not respond kindly. In April of 1775, British forces marched toward Concord, Massachusetts, with the intention of destroying the colonists' stockpile of weapons there. Some colonists tried to stop the British from advancing, and violence broke out between the colonists and British soldiers.

Shortly after this incident, the Continental Congress met once more with delegates from all 13 colonies present. The Second Continental Congress voted to raise a unified army against the British. A year later, on July 4, 1776, the Congress approved the Declaration of Independence, formally creating the United States of America.

The Declaration of Independence

The Declaration of Independence details the 13 colonies' reasons for wanting to separate from Great Britain and to form their own country. It contains these well-known lines:

> We hold these truths to be self-evident, that all men are created equal, that they are endowed by their Creator with certain unalienable Rights, that amongst these are Life, Liberty, and the pursuit of Happiness.

At the time, however, women did not have equal status as men, and these "certain unalienable Rights" did not apply to enslaved Africans or to American Indians.

The Declaration was written by Thomas Jefferson (right), who would later become the third president of the United States.

Articles of Confederation

The colonies won their independence through a long struggle called the American Revolutionary War. At the conclusion of the war, the colonies became 13 states, united as a country but each keeping a great deal of independence.

The new country needed a government. However, the Continental Congress did not want a government similar to Britain's, which had a **monarch.** Instead, the Congress decided to create a set of laws that limited the national government's power over the states and the people. The result was the Articles of Confederation. It governed the country from 1781 to 1789.

Under the Articles of Confederation, the national — or federal — government was a single legislative body made up of state representatives. Each state had one vote regardless of size or wealth. There was no single person at the head of the government.

The Articles of Confederation gave a lot of power to state governments and limited the federal government's powers. For example, the federal government had no way to raise taxes to pay the debts the country had **accumulated.** States could raise taxes but weren't obligated to provide the federal government with funds.

The federal government printed its own money, but the money was not worth much due to the fact that the nation was deep in debt and could not make income from taxes. Some states also printed their own money, but other states refused to recognize it, making those currencies worthless. Over time, the value of money dropped. The money people earned was worth little more than the paper on which it was printed.

Shays's Rebellion

The problems created by a limited federal government led to unhappiness. Daniel Shays was a Revolutionary War soldier who was angry over economic problems in his home state of Massachusetts. In 1787, he led more than 1,000 rebels who tried to take over an armory in Springfield, Massachusetts. Although the rebels were defeated, the event highlighted the problems caused by a limited federal government. Many state leaders began to think that a stronger central government was necessary.

Daniel Shays was arrested and sentenced for his actions, but he was eventually pardoned, or freed of all charges.

Drafting the Constitution

In 1787, a meeting of 55 delegates from 12 states was held in Philadelphia, Pennsylvania. The delegates met to discuss ways to improve the Articles of Confederation. However, many delegates wanted to create an entirely new structure of government. The delegates debated for a summer, drafted several different plans, and made many **compromises.** This meeting, which resulted in the creation of the Constitution, eventually became known as the Constitutional Convention.

The Virginia Plan

Virginia delegate James Madison was one of the delegates who supported the idea of creating a new government. He drafted the Virginia Plan, which became the foundation for the U.S. Constitution. Among other things, this plan proposed adding two more branches to the government in addition to the legislature: an executive branch and a judicial branch. Madison's plan was presented to the delegates by Edmund Randolph, the governor of Virginia.

For Your Information

Rhode Island was the only state that refused to send delegates to the Convention. It was vehemently against the idea of a new, stronger federal government.

Compromises

The Connecticut Compromise

While debating the Virginia Plan, the delegates began to argue over the subject of state representation. The Virginia Plan proposed that the number of representatives each state is allowed to have should depend on the state's population. Small states did not like this idea because it would mean they would have fewer votes in Congress. The New Jersey Plan was then proposed, which gave each state the same number of representatives. Large and small states battled over this issue.

Finally, a few delegates proposed the Great Compromise, also known as the Connecticut Compromise. This agreement cemented the two-house model of the U.S. Congress. In the Senate, each state would have the same number of representatives, called senators. In the House of Representatives, representation would be based on each state's population. This compromise promised that neither large states nor small states would have an unfair amount of power.

Terms and Limits

A term is the number of years elected officials can serve before they must run for election again. In the Senate, a term is six years. In the House of Representatives, a term is two years. Presidents serve four-year terms. In the judicial branch, there are no term restraints. Federal judges and justices can serve until their retirement, death, or removal from office by Congress through impeachment.

The Three-Fifths Compromise

In the 1780s, the practice of slavery was legal in most parts of the United States. A few Northern states had **abolished** slavery, but the Southern states still largely relied on slave labor to tend to their plantations. While the Constitution was being drafted, the issue of slavery divided many Northern and Southern delegates.

When it came time to determine the number of state representatives, slavery led to another debate. Northern delegates argued that enslaved people should not be included in the population as that would give the South more representatives and thus more power. It was feared that this power would further encourage the slave trade. However, Southern delegates felt they should be allowed to include enslaved people as part of their states' population. If the South could not count their enslaved population, then those states would not have as many votes in the House of Representatives. Eventually, the delegates reached an agreement called the Three-Fifths Compromise.

The South's profitable tobacco industry depended on the labor of enslaved African Americans.

The Three-Fifths Compromise stated that the enslaved population of a state could count as three fifths of the total white population of the state. This compromise benefited states with a large number of enslaved people, as it meant that they would have more representatives in Congress. For the Northern states, the Compromise ensured that the Southern states would agree to the Constitution and join the union to support a strong central government. The Compromise remained in effect until after the Civil War. Historians have argued that this law betrayed the ideal that "all men are created equal."

For Your Information

To **appease** the South in ways beyond the Three-Fifths Compromise, the Constitution also stated that Congress would not end the **importation** of enslaved people before 1808. On January 1, 1808, importing slaves into the country became illegal in the United States. However, slavery itself continued to be legal until 1865.

A Battle Over Rights

Drafting the Constitution was only the first step toward building a new government. In order for the Constitution to become the guiding document of the U.S. government, at least 9 out of the 13 states had to ratify it.

Supporters and Opponents

When the Convention ended in September 1787, the delegates returned home to inform the public about the Constitution. Some delegates rallied support for its ratification. These supporters were known as the Federalists.

However, not everyone wanted to ratify the Constitution. The opponents were called the Anti-Federalists. They thought the Constitution gave the federal government too much power over state governments. Anti-Federalists wanted the Constitution to specify the rights and liberties that were guaranteed to citizens.

The Declaration of Independence and the Constitution were both signed at Independence Hall in Philadelphia.

Several delegates saw the Constitution as flawed but still believed in its potential. Diplomat and founder Benjamin Franklin gave a speech on the last day of the Constitutional Convention. He said, "I agree to this Constitution with all its faults, if they are such; because I think a general Government necessary for us ... I doubt too whether any other Convention we can obtain, may be able to make a better Constitution."

Benjamin Franklin, at the age of 81, was the oldest delegate at the Constitutional Convention.

For Your Information

The Constitution of the United States has been in use longer than any other national constitution in the world.

The Federalists

To raise public support for the Constitution, founders Alexander Hamilton and James Madison, with the help of John Jay, wrote a series of essays known as the Federalist Papers. These 85 essays, published mainly in newspapers in New York State, detailed how the new government would work according to the Constitution.

The Federalist Papers became very **influential.** Not only did the essays explain the Constitution to the public, but they also successfully countered the Constitution's critics. The essays are still important today. They help scholars to understand the original intentions of the Constitution's writers.

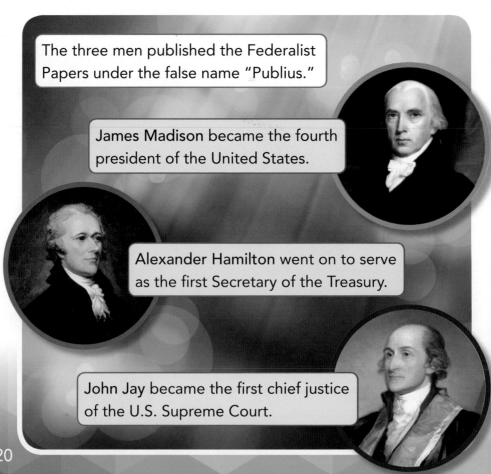

The three men published the Federalist Papers under the false name "Publius."

James Madison became the fourth president of the United States.

Alexander Hamilton went on to serve as the first Secretary of the Treasury.

John Jay became the first chief justice of the U.S. Supreme Court.

New Yorkers celebrate the Constitution's ratification with a float honoring Hamilton.

The Anti-Federalists

By January of 1788, five states had ratified the Constitution: Delaware, Pennsylvania, New Jersey, Georgia, and Connecticut. However, the ratification process continued to meet with resistance. Some states, such as Massachusetts, wanted **amendments** made to the Constitution, while Rhode Island simply rejected it.

Anti-Federalists were afraid that a strong federal government would lead to a type of government too similar to Great Britain's. They worried that the president might even become another monarch.

Patrick Henry

An early supporter of independence, Patrick Henry of Virginia was famed for his American Revolutionary war cry "Give me liberty or give me death!" He was also a leading opponent of the U.S. Constitution. Henry had even refused to attend the Constitutional Convention because he did not wish to show any support for the Constitution.

When the ratification debate began in Virginia, Henry spoke out against the Constitution. Like many other Anti-Federalists, Henry argued that in order to protect individual states and citizens, the Constitution needed to guarantee certain rights to the states and to the people.

Despite Henry's vocal opposition, after more than three weeks of debate, Virginia voted to ratify the Constitution. But Madison, who was also from Virginia, had heard Henry's and other Anti-Federalists' concerns. Madison went on to introduce a **bill** of rights to the Constitution.

Patrick Henry was known as an inspiring public speaker.

Opposing Beliefs and Demands

Federalist demands:
- A stronger central government
- Strong federal courts that could veto states
- A federal government that could raise taxes directly
- The Constitution

Who were the Federalists?
- Mostly businesspeople living in urban areas

Most prominent Federalists:
Alexander Hamilton, John Jay, John Adams, Benjamin Franklin, and James Madison

Anti-Federalist demands:
- More independent power for state governments
- Limited powers for federal courts
- States' rights to raise taxes
- A bill of rights

Who were the Anti-Federalists?
- Mostly small farmers living in rural areas

Most prominent Anti-Federalists:
Thomas Jefferson, James Monroe, Patrick Henry, Samuel Adams, and George Mason

George Mason was a vocal Anti-Federalist. He wrote the Virginia Declaration of Rights, which strongly influenced Madison's Bill of Rights.

Amending the Constitution

Four days before Virginia agreed to the Constitution, New Hampshire became the ninth state to ratify it on June 21, 1788. And so, the Constitution was officially established as the law of the new U.S. government. The following year, George Washington took office as the first president of the United States.

The Bill of Rights

Adding a bill of rights became one of the first tasks of the new government. Madison, who became a member of the House of Representatives, drafted 19 amendments to be added to the Constitution. These amendments outlined specific rights that the government would provide to the people. They also explained that the people would have certain rights that the government could not take from them. Only 10 of these amendments were finally approved.

On December 15, 1791, these 10 amendments became the Bill of Rights we know today. The Bill of Rights checks a strong central government by guaranteeing certain powers to the people.

The Bill of Rights

Amendment I

...w specting an establishment of religion, or prohibiting the free exercise thereof... ...of the people peaceably to assemble, and to petition the Government for...

Power of the People

Many amendments are still relevant today. For example, the First Amendment grants U.S. citizens freedom of religion, speech, and the press, as well as the right to peaceful assembly, which means the right to gather in protest.

Some amendments address problems that the colonists had faced when they were under British rule. For example, the Third Amendment states that in times of peace, it is illegal for soldiers to stay in a civilian's house without the owner's consent.

A few amendments protect the rights of people who have been accused of crimes. For example, the Sixth Amendment states that people have the right to a speedy trial, with judgment by an unbiased jury. This helps to ensure that citizens who are accused of crimes will not be kept in jail for a long time and that they will be judged fairly.

The final two amendments protect rights that are not mentioned within the Constitution. They say that citizens have more rights than just the ones explicitly stated in the Constitution. They also say that any power that is not granted to the federal government by the Constitution should be reserved for state governments or for the people themselves.

Legacy of the Constitution

The Constitution was designed to allow for change through the addition of amendments. Since the Bill of Rights was added to the Constitution, an additional 17 amendments have been ratified.

For about 100 years after the writing of the Declaration of Independence, only adult, white, male landowners could vote in some states. This injustice was corrected when the Thirteenth Amendment abolished slavery in 1865. Then, in 1870, the Fifteenth Amendment made it illegal to deny African American men the vote based on race. In 1920, the Nineteenth Amendment gave adult women the right to vote. In 1971, the Twenty-Sixth Amendment lowered the voting age from 21 to 18. Other amendments have been added to address how many terms a president can serve and who replaces a president who dies in office, among other issues.

Women's suffrage supporters march in celebration of the passing of the Nineteenth Amendment.

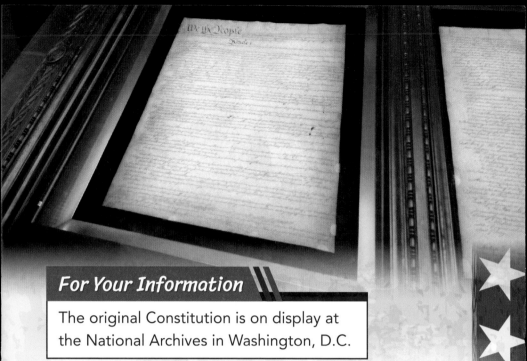

For Your Information

The original Constitution is on display at the National Archives in Washington, D.C.

It is not easy to make changes to the Constitution, but the nation's founders made sure that changes are indeed possible. For more than 200 years, constitutional amendments have been used to correct injustices in the law. Changes to the Constitution have granted important additional rights to U.S. citizens and have even redefined who can be a citizen.

When drafting the Constitution, the founders had to establish a strong federal government without taking too much power away from the states or the people. The Constitution might have its faults, as Benjamin Franklin acknowledged, but it is also undeniably important. Its ideals are so influential that many other nations, such as India and Japan, have modeled their constitution on the U.S. version. The Constitution is a document that has helped to define the role and legacy of the U.S. government.

GLOSSARY

abolish: to officially end or stop

accumulate: to gather over a period of time

amendment: a correction or an alteration

appease: to make happy

bill: an official list of things

compromise: an agreement that is made when both sides give up something

contrary: being in opposition to something

enforce: to carry out or make sure laws are being observed and obeyed

importation: the practice of bringing something into a country from a foreign country

influential: having the ability to bring about change

monarch: an unelected head of a country, such as a king or a queen

ratify: to officially approve through voting or signing

represent: to speak or serve on behalf of something or someone

---

INDEX